The Robin in the Tree

by **Dana Meachen Rau**

Reading Consultant: Nanci R. Vargus, Ed. D.

Marshall Cavendish
Benchmark
New York

Picture Words

 babies

 eggs

 grass

 nest

 robin (female)

 robin (male)

 robins

 sky

 sticks

 tree

 worm

 worms

A  sits in a .

The  flaps its wings.

The  flies through the ⬭.

The 🐦 lands on the ▭.

The 🐦 grabs a 🪱.

The 🪱 is food for the 🐦.

Next, the hops to a puddle.

The drinks the water.

Then the starts to sing.

A female hears its music.

The  flies to the

.

The finds a spot

for a .

The get
and mud.

They make a .

The mother  lays blue 🥚🥚🥚.

The mother 🐦 sits on the 🥚🥚🥚 in the 🪹.

The open in two weeks.

The bring to their .

Words to Know

flaps
　　to move wings up and down

flies
　　to travel through the sky

hops
　　to make small jumps

sing
　　to make music

Find Out More

Books

Atkins, Jeannine. *Robin's Home*. New York:
Farrar, Straus & Giroux, 2001.
Kottke, Jan. *From Egg to Robin*. Danbury, CT:
Children's Press, 2000.
Posada, Mia. *Robins: Songbirds of Spring*.
Minneapolis, MN: Carolrhoda Books, 2004.

Web Sites

Journey North: American Robin
http://www.learner.org/jnorth/search/Robin.html
Nature Works
http://www.nhptv.org/natureworks/robin.htm
American Robin
http://www.kidzone.ws/animals/birds/american-robin.htm

About the Author

Dana Meachen Rau is an author, editor, and illustrator. A graduate of Trinity College in Hartford, Connecticut, she has written more than one hundred books for children, including nonfiction, biographies, early readers, and historical fiction. She watches for robins every spring in her backyard in Burlington, Connecticut.

About the Reading Consultant

Nanci R. Vargus, Ed.D, used to teach first grade. Now she works at the University of Indianapolis. Nanci helps young people become teachers. Her class at Lynwood Elementary School in Indianapolis kept bird feeders full and recorded all the different birds that visited. Robins were a favorite!

Marshall Cavendish Benchmark
99 White Plains Road
Tarrytown, NY 10591-9001
www.marshallcavendish.us

All Internet sites were correct at the time of printing.

Library of Congress Cataloging-In-Data
Rau, Dana Meachen, 1971–
The robin in the tree / by Dana Meachen Rau.
    p.cm. — (Benchmark rebus)
Summary: "A rebus book that follows a robin's day"—Provided by publisher.
Includes bibliographical references.
ISBN-13: 978-0-7614-2304-1
ISBN-10: 0-7614-2304-4
Robins—Juvenile literature. I. Title. II. Series.
QL696.P288R38 2006
598.8'42—dc22   2005027378

Editor: Christine Florie
Editorial Director: Michelle Bisson
Art Director: Anahid Hamparian
Series Designer: Virginia Pope

Photo research by Connie Gardner

Rebus images, with the exception of the robins, provided courtesy of *Dorling Kindersley*.

Cover photo by *Dembinsky Photo Associates*/Jim Roetzel

The photographs in this book are used with permission and through the courtesy of:
Animals, Animals: p. 3 Ron Willocks, p. 11 Joyce & Frank Burek, p. 17 Daybreak Imagery; *Corbis*: p. 2 W. Perry Conway, p. 7 Arthur Morris, p.13 Peter Johnson, p. 15 Lynda Richardson; *Dembinsky Photo Associates*: p.19 Doug Locke; *Getty Images*: p. 5 Altrendo; *Peter Arnold*: p. 21 Alan & Sandy Carey; *Photo Researchers,Inc.*: p. 2 Millard H. Sharp, p. 9 Alan & Sandy Carey

Printed in Malaysia
1 3 5 6 4 2